Raised Bed Gardening
An Essential Guide for Beginners to Achieving a lot Through Raised Garden Beds

[Jaime Neil]

Copyright © 2019 Jaime Neil

All Rights Reserved. No portion of this book may be reproduced or used in any manner whatsoever without the expressed written permission of the author.

Table of Contents

Introduction 4

Chapter 1: Benefits of Using Raised Beds 7

Chapter 2: Raised Beds Tips and Tricks 16

Chapter 3: Planning Your Gardening 28

Chapter 4: The Fundamentals of Building Your Own Garden Beds 34

Chapter 5: Plants That Work Well in Raised Beds 44

Chapter 6: Raised Bed Garden Ideas 56

Chapter 7: Pest Control in Raised Beds 61

Chapter 8: Weed Control in Raised Beds 71

Chapter 9: Harvesting and Storing Your Bounties 77

Chapter 10: Disadvantages to Raised Bed Gardening .. 86

Conclusion 94

INTRODUCTION

Thank you for choosing my book; *Raised Bed Gardening: An Essential Guide for Beginners to Achieving a lot Through Raised Garden Beds*. This comprehensive guide will enlighten you on everything you need to know to start growing vegetables, edible flowers and herbs in raised beds.

Raised beds can be best described as a form of garden, constructed above the natural terrain. In raised bed gardening, the soil is usually formed in 3 to 4 feet wide beds bearing any size or shape. The soil is usually enclosed within a frame, typically made of rock, wood or blocks of concrete.

Raised bed gardening is the best option for those who want to grow a vegetable garden but are limited on space, as the yields are typically higher than flat ground gardens. Similarly, if your soil is not suitable for growing, adding quality soil into a raised bed garden provides a more economical solution. This is because you only add soil to the contained raised beds, rather than the whole area, including your pathways between plants. Overall, this form of gardening is the perfect choice for any less than perfect soil.

These gardens improve the growing condition of the plants by elevating their roots well above the poor-quality soil. As a bonus, it takes less effort to improve the soil into being a better growing medium for the plants.

You don't have to worry about your raised beds being infiltrated by certain "obnoxious" grass or tree roots (an aspect not typically seen in your average vegetable gardens) - this is because the soil used in raised bed gardening warms up faster during spring. In addition, the elevated position of raised beds prevents weed seeds from blowing into the garden soil.

CHAPTER 1: BENEFITS OF USING RAISED BEDS

1. No need for tilling: A raised bed gardening is a great way to set up the soil for the easiest gardening possible and does not require breaking ground immediately. Rather than tilling your soil from year to year in order to add fertilizer and make amendments, you can maintain your raised bed by simply adding your own fertile soil mix on top. Manures, mulches, compost, and other soil conditioners will directly go into the soil without tilling the soil. The soil can even do its own tilling as roots and worms push their way through the soil.

2. Higher yields: Since raised beds improve the condition of the soil, it will prevent the nematode problems linked with most soil - the microscopic worms can destroy your plants and reduce yields. In raised beds, you can easily plant more plants since you don't need the normal space between rows for walking. Vegetables planted in raised beds grow at higher densities just close enough to shade weeds and far apart enough to prevent overcrowding. And this usually results in higher yields.

3. Great for beginners: The raised bed gardening is a simple way of starting a garden since it removes many obstacles for beginners. Raised bed gardening may require a little investment initially but in most cases, there's a guaranteed success in the first year. Simply construct a box, add some soil, add some compost, add some seeds and some water, and something will surely grow. The raised bed gardening is much better than "Row crows" that requires tilling, fertilizing, tilling again, seeding, weeding and weeding – the process is not as easy as that of raised bed.

4. Reduces back pain: It is astonishing how much back pain and knee strain weeding a garden can give you. However, a raised bed garden, particularly the ones that are about 12-inch tall can prevent back and joint ache. Therefore, it is a great idea to consider raised bed gardening as an investment to your health.

5. Prevents contaminated soil: Gardeners in the urban areas have a higher possibility of consuming heavy metals which includes lead since various vegetables like greens, tomatoes, and roots absorb heavy metals from soils that are already contaminated and this can lead to a real threat. Although, placing your beds away from the road, planting thick hedges and carrying out research on the past uses of your land can all help, raised beds offer the exceptional opportunity to use new soil that has not been contaminated with toxicity. You can also reduce toxicity by adding compost – to bind heavy metals to soil particles and dilute the concentrations of contamination from year to year.

6. Raised beds can be temporary: Tenants who desire to have a raised bed garden need to discuss with their landlords by showing them a lovely picture of a raised bed garden. A tidy, neat and well-built garden box can help to improve property values rather than being an eyesore. However, if the landlord refuses, then you can build a temporary garden by making use of a removable garden box. Simply set the box on the ground, place cardboard over the grass inside, and fill the box with soil. So that when you relocate, you can easily take the box with you and spread out the soil as well as throwing down the grass seed again.

7. You can create raised bed earlier in the season: This is mostly accredited to better drainage in the soil – planting early in raised bed gardens is achievable since the soil dry out more quickly in the spring and warms faster for planting than the soil at the ground level. Most gardeners often find that a great number of plants have overwintered in a raised bed garden and most of this has to do with kind of soil used for the raised bed. If you untilled your soil and strengthen with compost, it'll normalize temperatures compare to disturbed, nutrient-poor soil.

8. Reduces weeds and crabgrass: In actual fact, tilling leads to more weeds by hiding weed seeds and providing them the ideal opportunity to proliferate. Successful gardeners of raised beds confirm that covering raised beds with black plastic, cardboard, or mulch in the spring helps to kill all the weeds that grew during winter. So, when it is time to begin planting again, just rake off the dead weeds to prevent them from germinating. A raised bed garden is one of the most effectual methods of battling crabgrass. Simply set up a weed barrier underneath the beds at least ten inches high to prevent the grasses from penetrating.

9. Raising your soil means better drainage: In a marshy yard or an area that is prone to flood, a raised bed garden may be the only option to having a full growing season. 11 inches is the most popular depth for a raised bed garden and that's enough drainage for most crops. This also provides the plants with almost a foot of extra breathing room above wet conditions. Generally, raised bed gardens enable better drainage, even in heavy rains.

10. Keeps out critters: Even though slugs can climb, the tall sides of a raised bed box help to slow them down and gives you the opportunity to stop them in their track. Many growers confirm that slugs cannot crawl over the copper flashing that borders many raised bed boxes. You can also stop crawling critters such as groundhogs from stealing root crops by fixing a hardware cloth underneath the raised bed box. Dogs are less likely to urinate directly on your plants due to the height of the raised beds. To keep deer away, simply buy a box with a built-deer fence or add the deer fencing directly to your raised bed.

CHAPTER 2: RAISED BEDS TIPS AND TRICKS

Let's summarize some of the main points about raised beds and give you some tips to ensure your beds are productive and easy to maintain. When built correctly, raised beds reduce your workload and increase your productivity, so let's ensure you get the most from your beds.

Build-up Your Soil

Preparing the soil is the key to success with raised bed gardening, you need a good six to twelve inches of high quality, organically rich soil so that it encourages the development of healthy plants. Raised beds help you get past issues with poor quality soil and, when prepared properly, allow you to plant your produce more densely than you can in normal soil, meaning more vegetables from the same growing area.

Planting and maintaining a raised bed takes a lot less time so combine this with the increased yield and you are going to produce a large number of vegetables! Because the higher planting density shades out weeds and you will have less work to do plus watering and harvesting is more efficient.

We discussed the soil mix earlier in this book. You need to ensure you create the best possible soil mix you can afford. There is nothing wrong with using what you have at hand and then over the next year building up the beds and replacing the soil as you can afford to buy more compost or get hold of more manure.

Think About Spacing

How you space your plants will influence the quantity and even the quality of your produce. Applying the principles of square foot gardening means you get a much higher yield out of your beds. Another strategy is hexagonal planting where you offset the rows which allow for a closer planting density between rows.

Remember though that planting some crops too close together will reduce the yield. One researcher discovered that planting romaine lettuces 10" apart instead of the usual 8" resulted in a doubling of the harvest weight. Tight spacing can make your plants more susceptible to pests and diseases, but keeping a close eye on your plants will enable you to take preventative measures before the problem gets too serious.

Growing Upwards

Growing vegetables vertically enables you to really maximize your use of space and increase your harvest. Vertical gardening is a very exciting development and plants such as onions, strawberries, radishes, lettuce and more are ideal candidates for vertical gardening, meaning you can get even more out of your raised beds.

Try training vine crops up trellises along one side of your raised beds and you will find that you can get even more out of your raised beds.

Interplanting

This is a fantastic way for you to increase the productivity of your raised beds. Plant your corn, beans, and squash together or tomatoes, basil and onions or beets and celery or onions, radishes and carrots. All of these combinations work well together and allow you to significantly increase your yield. You will be surprised just how much you can grow in a few raised beds that are managed correctly.

Succession Planting

There's another great way to increase your yield whilst reducing waste. Rather than plant all your lettuces (for example) at once, you plant a few every couple of weeks, meaning you get a continual supply of lettuce throughout the growing season. You can often get three, four or even five crops from a single area whilst significantly reducing the amount of wastage.

Extending Your Growing Season

Raised beds allow you to extend your growing season because they are naturally warmer than the surrounding soil. However, you can also easily turn your raised bed into a cold frame or cover it with fleece using some of the techniques detailed earlier in this book. This allows you to extend your growing season and get even more out of your raised beds.

Of course, the same techniques can be used to start your plants off earlier on! If you cover your soil with black plastic sheeting around six to eight weeks before the last frost date, it will heat the soil. You then cover the soil with a clear plastic tunnel and when the soil hits 65-70°F; you cover the black plastic with straw and put your plants in place. The straw stops the plastic from heating too much whilst the plastic retains moisture and heat. When the weather has warmed sufficiently you then remove the plastic tunnel.

Don't Walk on the Soil

If you walk on the soil you will compact it, which then means it is harder for you to weed, harvest and plant. The idea is that the soil in a raised bed is light and fluffy which is perfect for your plants. Ensure you build your raised beds to such a size that you can reach all parts of it from the edge. If you have inherited raised beds and they are just that little bit too big then use some paving slabs or boards so that you can easily reach parts without compacting too much soil.

Mulch after Planting

When you have planted out your raised bed it will be more densely planted than normal. However, adding a mulch of straw, compost or wood chips will help retain moisture and prevent weeds from growing. Avoid using leaves as these can bring pests and diseases on to your bed and avoid grass clippings as they can clump, retaining too much moisture which will then damage your plants.

Integrate Your Irrigation System

Drip irrigation and soaker hoses are two of the best ways to irrigate your raised beds and if you integrate this from the start then you can save yourself a lot of work later on.

Top Dress with Compost

Every year you need to add a couple of inches of compost or well-rotted manure to your raised beds which will help replenish the nutrients and beneficial micro-organisms in the soil. Some people will replace the soil completely every couple of years but that isn't necessary if you look after it properly. It is expensive to do and should only be done if there has been a build-up of pests or diseases in the soil.

Fluff the Soil Regularly

The soil in your raised beds will naturally compact a little over time. Every now and then, when you see it compacting use a fork or hand fork to fluff up and loosen the soil.

Cover Unused Beds

If you aren't using a bed for a while, for whatever reason then you need to cover the bed with a tarp or black plastic sheeting. This will prevent weeds from growing and will help to stop your soil from compacting.

You can plant green manure crops overwinter to cover the soil if you like, though you will have to dig them in the coming spring. It's a personal choice, so decide which you want to do.

Regularly Maintain Your Beds

By spending a little time every year (usually over the winter months) maintaining and repairing your raised beds, you can extend their lifespan significantly. It will save you a lot of work in the long term and ensures your beds remain productive and in good condition.

CHAPTER 3: PLANNING YOUR GARDENING

The key to successful raised garden beds is planning out your garden. This need not be stressful but does require taking a little time to assess a variety of considerations. It is well worth sketching out your garden to determine the best location and size of beds. Ideally, you should look to have the long side of each bed facing south for maximum exposure to light. If you have the narrow end facing south, you may find that taller plants limit the amount of sunlight allowed for smaller plants at the back.

Plan out your garden but remember to allow a generous amount of space between each bed to allow for paths. If you are planning on having grass between the beds, be sure to allow enough space to accommodate your lawn mower. Even if you are planning on paving the paths, you need to ensure that you have sufficient space to move a wheelbarrow between the beds. You can minimize the maintenance of the paths by using a membrane underneath the flagstones to reduce the risk of weeds.

Consider the material you will use for your raised beds. Most traditional types of raised bed are made from cedar. The reason for this is that the wood is naturally resistant to rot. However, there are other materials available for your raised beds such as composite or recycled plastic which may be more appropriate for your garden. You can also use other materials such as flags, which can be painted or decorated to complement your garden aesthetic.

Add a trellis to your raised beds. Most raised beds are sufficiently sturdy to support a trellis system. This allows for support for climbing flowers or vegetables such as beans. There are many types of trellis which can be attached to your bed without visible holes and the potential to relocate the trellis to other beds.

Before you begin planting or growing, you will need to also plan and prepare the garden. If the ground is new to gardening, you should double dig the area for the bed to at least a depth of sixteen inches. This will allow you to pull any stones and to check the soil composition. You can also check for any signs of roots in the bed area. This will show if you need a root barrier for living trees such as a heavy plastic sheet. If you pile the soil up in the center of the area you will be able to set the new raised bed into place without needing further digging.

If you have had an issue with burrowing animals in your garden, you will also need to plan for this. Most burrowing pest problems can be overcome by using a half inch layer of hardware cloth before you add the soil. The edges of the raised bed are overlapped by the mesh to a height of at least three or four inches. Stapling in the cloth will prevent it from being disturbed.

When you are planning out the beds, be sure to check that they are completely level. Ensure the soil is spread out evenly and level. Once you have added the soil, avoid stepping in the bed. When you step into the bed, you will compact the soil and cause aeration to be reduced. You should also train your pets to stay out of the raised bed or plan to have the beds in an area not accessible by the pets.

When planning out your raised bed garden, you can allow your creativity to shine. The beds can be arranged in meticulous rows or into a geometric pattern. If you have an abundance of space, you can plan your raised beds into a real garden feature.

CHAPTER 4: THE FUNDAMENTALS OF BUILDING YOUR OWN GARDEN BEDS

Most people consider the best element of establishing a raised bed garden is building your own garden beds. Building raised beds can be simple and easy. However, it is important to get the fundamentals right.

What wood should you use?

The most preferred choice of wood for building a raised bed is cedar. Cedar is naturally resistant to rot. This means that your cedar raised bed has a life expectancy of at least ten to fifteen years. However, if cedar is a little outside of your price range, you could consider spruce or pine. These are not likely to have the extensive lifespan of cedar but should last for at least five or six years before being compromised by damage from rot. It is important that whatever wood you choose, it is untreated. The chemicals used in wood treatments can leach into the soil and potentially into your vegetables, fruits or plants.

How tall should your bed be?

You can build your raised beds to any height of your choosing. Generally, raised beds have a maximum height of thirty-six inches. The most popular height of a raised bed is eleven inches and can be achieved by stacking two 2"x6" boards. Regardless of the chosen height of your raised bed, the plants will still be able to have their roots below the surface of the ground under the bed. If you choose to have a higher sided bed, you should bear in mind that the additional soil used to fill a taller bed will have greater weight. To compensate for this additional pressure, you will need to install cross supports. The choice of how tall to make your raised beds will greatly depend on how you intend to use the bed. For example, if you wish to grow root vegetables, you will need additional depth. However, if you are looking to ease back pain when gardening, you will need to consider your comfortable height to work with.

How long and wide should your bed be?

This again will depend on your personal preferences. However, it is recommended that you restrict the width of a raised bed to a maximum of four feet. This allows you to reach the middle of the bed comfortably from either side. Most people choose a length based on the length of timber used.

The process of building your own raised garden beds:

Building your own raised beds can actually be accomplished in just six simple steps. This is relatively easy for those with some basic DIY skills.

Step One: Mark it out:

Determine how big your raised bed will be. If you are planning to make your garden filled with raised beds, it is better to plan it out on paper in advance. Rake the ground to ensure that it is level and use string to mark out the potential bed.

Step Two: Build the walls:

Start with your corner posts. A good size is twelve-inch sections of four by four boards. Screw the side boards onto the corner post and stack the boards on top. Be sure to keep the boards even against the sides of the corner posts. You should ensure that you check if the corners are at right angles using an angle square.

Step Three: Connect up the walls:

Connect the side walls with the outsides of the corner posts.

Step Four: Check its square:

Once all the walls are connected, check the raised bed is square by measuring both diagonals. If the measurements are the same, the raised bed is square, if not you will need to adjust accordingly.

Step Five: Ensure it's sturdy:

Use 2x2 stakes to reinforce the outer walls. You will need to pound the stakes into the ground. Use deck screws to secure the stake. Repeat this on each of the four walls.

Step Six: Fill the bed:

Once your raised bed is built, you will need to fill it. You can use topsoil from your garden or increase the nutrient content using peat moss or compost. Once the raised bed is filled with soil, water the bed well before you begin planting.

Maintaining Your Raised Bed

One of the advantages of raised bed gardening is that it is very easy to maintain. However, there're some normal maintenance practices you need to follow:

Water

Raised bed soil tends to warm more quickly and dries out faster than the soil at ground level. Therefore, there is a need for you to water your beds on a regular basis. Make use of irrigation during dry seasons to supplement natural rainfall. You can place drip irrigation or soaker hoses directly on your raised beds. You can also consider using overhead sprinklers but if they get the plant foliage wet, there's the possibility of spreading diseases.

Fertilize

Fertilization of plants grown traditionally is similar to that of raised bed gardens. For the majority of crops, a complete fertilizer that is applied at the rate of 1-2 pounds per hundred square feet is okay. You can also apply manures and organic fertilizers. Use the recommendations based on soil tests for more specific fertilizer information. And when you want to choose fertilizer, go for the ones that have 2% phosphorus or less. However, edibles may need more phosphorus – a soil test will help in determining that.

Use Mulch

Using mulch helps to keep the soil moist and the weeds down. You can make use of organic mulches like hay or straw, or wood chips placed on landscape fabric. Under organic mulches, weed growth is repressed, less water is lost through evaporation, and the soil temperatures are lower. And all these make it much easier to maintain your raised beds.

Clean up your beds

You can till your vegetable plants back into your raised beds at the end of a growing season. This will help to add organic matter in the soil although extra compost can be added for more nutrients. The soil will get improved over time so that you won't need to till again.

CHAPTER 5: PLANTS THAT WORK WELL IN RAISED BEDS

Raised bed gardening is becoming more and more popular in order to take maximum advantage of small spaces. If you plan your raised bed garden correctly, you can get amazing crops of vegetables, flowers, and herbs with very little effort compared to what you must do in traditional gardening.

These types of gardens have an important role in the landscape of the home. They feature framed areas above the ground and often have wooden frames around the area. They have an increased ability to drain away excess water and eliminate compacted soil. In addition, you can add soil nutrients as necessary to help your plants be the best they can be. This allows gardeners to plant a variety of plants in their garden.

Most plants will work well in raised bed gardens. The exception is those plants that are large or have very deep roots or sprawling top growth. Other plants that don't work in raised beds are those that are top-heavy and tall and therefore need to be firmly anchored.

Since the plants in your raised beds will be sharing soil, light, fertilizer, and water, you should make sure to choose plants with similar or the same requirements for growth and development.

As far as size, moderately tall plants work well. Also, trailing plants or smaller plants work quite well in raised bed gardens and can be planted together. Planting in raised beds is just another type of container gardening, and therefore basically requires you to follow the same rules. Plant the trailing plants along the edges, so they spill over.

Vegetables are pretty easy to grow in raised beds. You can maximize the amount of yield you get from your crops by planting the summer plants as soon as the spring ones have been harvested and fall ones as soon as the summer ones have been harvested. Since the fertilizer and soil are easier to control, you can plant vegetables and plants closer together than in a traditional garden.

In addition, raised bed gardens are being used to raise tropical houseplants as annuals. As far as flowering plants go, you can raise both annuals and perennials in your raised garden. You should choose annuals that match the availability of sunlight in your area. The growing conditions offered in the raised bed garden seriously increase the growth of the annuals. Annuals will flourish in the rich soil offered in the raised bed garden.

Perennials will give your garden a more permanent addition. They will flower year after year and can form the basis for your raised bed garden. You can add perennials to create a low maintenance garden that requires very little work through the seasons. To achieve constant color and flowering, you should choose plants that bloom at various times of the year.

Raised bed gardens are great for vegetable gardening because they offer a neat area for planting. The rich soil will ensure that you have a prosperous harvest, providing that you have placed them in such a way that there is room for growth. Make sure that you read all your labels so that you can decide on the best placement for the plants. An added benefit of the raised bed garden is that it keeps pests out- the frame provides a base to which you can place poles to attach fencing.

Peas

Peas work well in raised garden beds, according to the National Gardening Association. The raised design helps drain the excess water away and allows gardeners to plant earlier. You should plant peas after the last frost of the winter.

Peppers

According to the National Gardening Association, peppers grow quite well in raised bed gardens, especially if they're really wet. This is because of the drainage and the warmer temperatures offered by raised bed gardens. It's best to plant them after the last spring frost, but they can be started inside earlier and then moved outside in order to create an earlier harvest.

Eggplant

Like peppers, raised beds are great for growing eggplants. Eggplants have beautiful purple flowers that make your vegetable garden especially attractive.

Okra

Okra grows quite well in raised beds and does really well next to peppers and eggplants. According to the National Gardening Association, you should plant okra from a seed. It doesn't do well with frost and doesn't do well in a really hot climate either.

Potatoes

Potatoes do not only perform well in a raised bed, they are also very easy to harvest. Potatoes benefits from hilling the soil around the shoots as they develop. Raised bed garden enable you to contain your hills easily and even make a bed that you can add to as your plant grow. Potatoes require loose, loamy soil that drains well and they grow perfectly when they're can spread out easily in the soil. Loose soil also prevents potatoes from rotting. You are sure to harvest higher yields with bigger tubers from your raised bed garden.

Tomatoes

Tomatoes are heavy feeders that require nutrient-dense soil to flourish. Therefore, you need to customize your soil by adding additional compost. The only disadvantage, however, is that it is difficult for tomato cages and stakes to stand up in the loose soil.

Onions

There're 3 major reasons onions grow well in raised beds — they need a long growing season, they require lots of organic matter, and they love quick-draining soil. The warmer soil in raised beds gives onions a head start. Naturally, raised bed soils can be prepared to suit your needs; therefore you can add plenty of compost to your beds if you want to plant onions. It takes more hundred days for the seeds of onion to mature and if reside anywhere with 4 seasons, you will want to give the onions the longest time in your garden.

Leafy greens

Leafy greens like kale, spinach, and lettuce perform wonderfully in raised beds. These crops should be planted immediately you get a trowel into your soil. Because raised bed soils warm faster than the ground means you start planting earlier and harvest a lot before the summer period. Leafy greens don't do well with mushy roots, therefore the fast draining soil of your raised bed will ensure your lovely greens will not stand in water for too long.

Root vegetables

It is essential to have complete control over the soil when planting crops for their root. You get to fill your raised beds with the perfect soil that suit your need – soil free of debris, clay, and rocks that could lead to misshapen vegetables or obstruct the growth of roots. Parsnips, radishes, beets, and carrots do well in loose, rock-free soil where there's enough space for them to spread out.

Other great additions to raised bed gardens are herbs. They grow just as well as the vegetables and annuals will. The extra organic material and the soil looseness allow the roots to spread quite nicely. When the roots spread, the plant can better absorb nutrients and moisture from the soil. Herbs can be paired with vegetables or annuals or can be planted all on their own. You should disperse those strong-smelling herbs throughout the garden to repel insects. In addition, you will attract bees and butterflies, which will keep the pests to a minimal level.

CHAPTER 6: RAISED BED GARDEN IDEAS

Plants require more oxygen, which is vital to their growth. Also, since you create your own soil mixture you can use the proper mixture for each of your plants, which will yield healthier, larger vegetables and flowers. The basis for a raised garden bed is to elevate it up from the ground and contain it in walls or other containers. Your only limit is your imagination. The following are some suggestions for your raised bed garden.

Build a Multi-Level Raised Bed

Instead of building rectangle or square beds and putting them beside each other, you can add some visual appeal to your garden by creating a raised garden with several different levels. Build one that's four foot high then one around it that's three foot high in the same shape and diameter. This gives your garden a layered look. You can also build several different large beds and then build some smaller beds in different shapes and sizes. Place the smaller ones on top of the large ones.

Create a Courtyard Using Raised Garden Beds

You can build up your raised garden beds around seating in your yard or garden. Create a beautiful courtyard escape by building the raised beds so that they are tall enough. Create a single bed or a "u" shaped one surrounding the seating area to conceal it. A stone or block bed can double as seating as well.

Make sure that you place bright, beautiful flowers in the beds. If the seating doubles as a picnic area, you can consider planting produce as well.

Raised Bed Gardens on Slopes

If part of your yard is on a slope, you can utilize the space better with raised garden beds. Build standard beds, and then use bricks or blocks to prop up the side of the bed that is on the slope. You should dig out part of the ground under the bricks so that they will be tightly wedged. Then, when you fill it with topsoil, only a little will escape from the bottom of the bed. You can design the raised beds into a stair step way down the slope.

CHAPTER 7: PEST CONTROL IN RAISED BEDS

In traditional gardening, many of the pests that attack your plants are soil borne. If you are planting in new soil, your plants are bothered a lot less by both pests and diseases. If you are reusing soil then there is a chance that some pests or diseases will be transferred with the soil.

Pest control in a raised bed is similar to traditional gardening in that you take the same steps to control the pests.

Slugs and Snails

One of the biggest problems you are going to face will be slugs and snails. These are the gardener's worst enemy and will devour your seedlings and plants without hesitation.

Keeping these pests away is tricky but the first step is to make sure that you do not provide them anywhere to hide. If you ensure there is no debris on the paths or in the beds then they have less space to get out of the way and are more likely to stay away or be eaten by predators. Use good straw mulch rather than fallen leaves, which will just give them somewhere to hide.

Beer traps work though they will not catch all of the slugs and snails, they will catch a lot. They need changing every couple of days, especially after it has rained, and will stink to high heaven on a hot day. Ensure the lip of the trap is about an inch above ground level to stop beneficial insects such as beetles from falling into it.

Slug pellets work well, killing off the majority of slugs, though there are concerns regarding the safety of using them with respect to pets, children and beneficial wildlife. After rain showers, you need to put down fresh pellets to ensure they keep working.

All the other tricks such as crushed eggshells, copper bands and the like don't particularly work. They may deter some but the hardier pests will get across your barrier and still eat your plants. The most effective method of deterring pests is bramble sticks. These have thorns on them which slugs and snails do not like crossing. Cut some brambles down and circle your plants with these cuttings to help keep these voracious pests at bay.

Because the soil is good quality and regularly amended you will find that you won't suffer from soil-borne pests as much. If you practise crop rotation then you are going to minimize the build-up of these pests, reducing potential problems in future years.

Carrot Fly

To protect your beds from carrot fly you can either plant onion, leeks or garlic with the carrots (which puts them off as the flies can't smell the carrots) or you can attach a fine mesh "fence" to your raised bed about two feet high. Carrot flies do not typically go above eighteen inches off the ground so this simple barrier will generally keep them off.

Building a planter two or three feet off the ground will also help keep off carrot flies. Try not to disturb the soil around your carrots as this lets the carrot aroma free, which will attract carrot flies. Most commonly, they are attracted after thinning out your carrots as this releases the fragrance of carrot, which these flies can smell from a long way away.

Aphids

Aphids may well be a problem, depending on what you are growing. They blow in on the wind or just arrive under their own steam. When you are tending your beds and watering your plants you need to check your plants for any sign of disease or pests. Aphids can easily be dealt with if they are caught early on and only become a problem when they aren't seen and multiply like crazy. You can use a variety of sprays; though ensure that whatever you choose is safe for use on food crops as not all sprays are.

A common sign of aphid infestation is lots of ants around your plants. Ants farm aphids and you will see them going up and down your plants to the aphids where they feed on the sweet secretions from the aphids.

You can reduce aphid infestations by planting trap or sacrificial crops in the area. Nasturtiums are a popular trap crop as aphids love feeding on this plant. Simply plant it around the borders of your vegetable garden and then regularly remove and destroy the aphids to stop them spreading.

Encouraging Natural Predators

You can help minimize problems with pests by encouraging natural predators onto your vegetable plot. Planting flowering herbs such as marjoram, chives, lavender, and rosemary will encourage flying predators that will eat aphids and other pests.

Putting a "bug hotel" on your plot will give these predators somewhere to live so they can do their job, reducing the number of pests on your plot.

Another great idea is to build a small pond on your plot, which could be as simple as sinking a washing up bowl into the ground and filling it with water. This will encourage frogs and toads which will eat slugs and other pests. Just remember to put bricks in the bowl so that your friendly predators can get in and out easily enough.

The other advantage of encouraging wildlife onto your plot is that the flying insects are often pollinators which are vital if you want your vegetables to produce fruit.

Year after year I hear from people complaining that their pumpkins or apple trees or whatever haven't produced any fruit and I find out they don't have any flowers in their vegetable patch to encourage pollinators in! I have now dedicated an entire raised bed to flowers because it will encourage beneficial insects to visit my plot, plus I have flowering herbs in pots scattered around the paths. I move these around depending on what needs pollinating to help give nature that little bit of extra encouragement.

If you are growing brassicas and other vegetables loved by caterpillars then you must net the beds with a tight weave mesh. You need to build a frame for your beds and you just need to put a fine mesh netting over this. Make sure the netting is very fine and you don't accidentally buy strawberry netting or pea netting, both of which have holes large enough for a butterfly to get through. Netting can also be used to protect crops from birds too.

Raised beds suffer a lot less from pests than traditional gardening. Slugs and snails are best minimized by giving them nowhere to hide and vigilance is your best defence against many other pests. Encouraging natural predators is by far the best way to keep pest numbers down and you are also giving local wildlife a much-needed home.

CHAPTER 8: WEED CONTROL IN RAISED BEDS

In raised bed gardening you typically use sterile soil and a compost mix in your bed, which means there are fewer weeds in your beds. However, sometimes there are seeds in the manure we use or seeds blow into our raised beds. In my case, I inherited a plot with six foot high weeds in the raised beds. You may even re-use soil from somewhere else in your garden or use non-sterile soil, meaning you are more likely to get weeds.

Because the soil is not compacted it is very easy to remove any weeds that do appear, you just carefully pull them out, making sure you have got all of the root (particularly with any perennial weeds). These can then be burnt or composted.

Whilst you can resort to weed killer you need to be very careful because it can blow on to your vegetable plants or the toxins can be absorbed by them from the soil. If you find large dandelions in awkward places where you can't get the roots out then a large pinch of salt in the middle will not only kill the leaves but the root too.

My preferred solution with weeds is to tackle them before they become a problem. If you are creating new raised beds then this is your best solution and it will mean the time you spend maintaining your beds is minimal. Two or three times a week, walk around your raised beds with a hoe and just knock the top of any weed seedlings off. You can leave them on the soil and they will break down, though any perennial weed seedlings (e.g. dandelion and dock) should be removed and disposed of. It is best to do this in the morning on a warm, dry day as the weeds will dry out and die.

This doesn't take long to do and it makes a huge difference in maintaining your plot and keeping it looking great. Plus, if you keep the weeds down you find there are fewer places for pests such as slugs and snails to hide.

I used to have a vegetable plot that was 15 x 5 yards in size and I didn't particularly have a slug and snail problem because the soil was bare between the plants. Everyone used to wonder how it looked so good and how I kept it so neat when they spent hours weeding their plots. The secret was I hoed the plot regularly. Three times a week, I would spend no more than 20 minutes hoeing the plot and taking down the baby weeds and they would never get a chance to establish themselves. For me, this is a huge timesaver and you'd be wise to invest in a hoe if you don't already own one.

When you are not using a bed for a while, such as overwinter, or you have just built it and haven't decided what to put in it yet then you should cover the bed to prevent weeds growing. You can use tarps if you want, though black garbage bags, split along the seams and then stapled to the edging boards makes for a great, and cheap solution, though they are easily damaged in high winds. You can see I have used this method in the picture above. Ensure you use strong bags as the cheaper ones are thin and will be damaged in high winds. These beds had been harvested, weeded and had manure dug in, then I covered them with split garbage bags. The stones are there to weigh down the joins where the bags weren't quite big enough to stretch the width of the bed.

CHAPTER 9: HARVESTING AND STORING YOUR BOUNTIES

Harvesting is the glory of gardening. There are some tips that can ensure you attain a bountiful harvest and successful storage to lengthen the lifespan of your harvest into fall or over winter for some vegetables. It is best to harvest from your garden early in the morning, just after the dew has dried. This is due to the fact that the crops are crisper, cooler and have a higher content of water more than they do in the warmer part of the day.

Potatoes

Your potatoes are ready to be harvested when the plants wilt and die. Make use of a pitchfork to reduce damage during harvest – work your fork in from the side and get under the plant very well before you lift up to expose the potatoes.

Tomatoes

You can harvest your tomatoes when they start to turn red. Check the plants daily and pick the red, firm tomatoes. Tomatoes should be harvested with the calyx on. And you can harvest the unripe tomatoes too – windfalls or late-season, simply set the unripe tomatoes in a warm place indoors and they will turn red. You can also wrap them up individually in newspaper and store in a cool room that's dark to enable slower ripening.

Onions

To harvest onions, let the stalks turn yellow, then bend them down and wait for two weeks. After that, stick a pitchfork well under the onion bulbs and lift up soil gently to loosen the soil around the onion bulbs. Then, you need to wait for another two weeks before harvest – this technique will help to increase the size of your onions.

Squash

Squash should be kept dry as they near maturity. When squash lies in moist soil or grass, it can develop small rot spots that will make it difficult for it to be stored for winter. Some gardeners always place a small saucer beneath every squash to keep them dry. You can also trellis the squash by tying each matured squash to the trellis with a piece of nylon or netting strip which is designed like a sling to hold the heavy squash.

Broccoli

Ensure you harvest your broccoli before any small yellow flowers appear on the central cluster. Start by picking the main center and then cut it 5 inches down the central stalk to enable the side shoots to grow into new smaller heads that you can harvest frequently for weeks or even months. When you harvest the small heads continuously just before they develop any flower, it will help triple your yield from each plant. And this technique will lengthen your harvest for months if the weather condition is favorable.

Storing

To successfully store your vegetables, you need to take the following factors into consideration.

Temperature: Cool temperatures of about 32 – 55°F prevents the loss of moisture and delays fungi and bacteria growth that spoil crops. Use warmer temperatures to enhance the speed of ripening for a bunch of green tomatoes.

Moisture: Vegetables that are stored tend to wither faster and lose value without appropriate moisture. The storage location should have the moisture that reaches about 80% to 90% relative humidity that is suitable for most vegetables. Wet sand, damp burlap bags and layers of moist sphagnum moss will help to increase moisture.

Ventilation: Harvested vegetables still "breathe" and need sufficient oxygen to retain high quality. Tissue breakdown and wilting are reduced by appropriate circulation of air.

Whether you want to store your bounties whole, dry or freeze-preserve them, it is best to find out the kind of storage that is suitable for the crops. The following suggestions will help you get started:

- Vegetables can be segmented into the following storage group: cool-moist for potatoes and other root crops, dry for beans and peas, cool-dry for onions, and warm-dry for pumpkin and squash.
- Vegetables like winter squash, pumpkin, onions, and garlic should not be stored in the fridge. A dark place at 50 – 60°F and normal dampness are suitable for them.
- Root crops such as turnips, potatoes, parsnips, carrots, and beets can be left for a

part or all of the winter in the garden you grew them. And when the ground starts to freeze, cover the vegetables with hay, straw or leaf mulch for protection.

- You can store onions, leeks, kale, cauliflower, Chinese cabbage, cabbage, and beets under mulch during fall frosts. Brussels sprouts, which can withstand some light freezing, can be left in the garden for many months.

- Sweet potatoes, winter squash, onions, and potatoes need a curing period to improve their storage qualities.

- You can refrigerate vegetables that have high water content like cucumbers, carrots, all members of the cabbage family and leafy greens once you harvest them.

Tip: There are certain vegetables that should never be stored with apple since apples tend to release a substance called ethylene gas. Ethylene makes carrots to taste bitter and shorten the storage life of pumpkins and Irish potatoes.

CHAPTER 10: DISADVANTAGES TO RAISED BED GARDENING

Though raised bed gardening has many advantages, there are also some disadvantages that come with it. The disadvantages include: losing moisture quickly, portability, cost and limits on the equipment you can use.

Moisture Issues

Since raised beds are up off the ground, they tend to lose moisture quickly. Since they are elevated, the soil is exposed to winds that dry it out and it gets more sun, which promotes rapid evaporation of water. They also drain really well, which causes them to lose moisture to the soil under the bed. If you mulch the bed with straw, wood chips, or even plastic, you can reduce the amount of moisture loss from the sun and wind. In addition, you will most likely need to water more frequently in drier, hotter climates to help counteract the loss of water in the raised bed garden.

Circulation of Air

Since the plants are grown more closely together than in a traditional garden, there is a probability that they won't' receive the right amount of air and oxygen. When plants don't get the air they need to survive, they may end up dying because they could end up getting diseases, or they may rot.

Hard to Move

Raised beds are pretty permanent, and therefore if you need to move them it can be a bit of a hassle. It is difficult to take a raised bed apart if you need to move it to a new location or remove it altogether. Also, since it is permanent, it can make it difficult to expand or shrink your garden according to your needs. Beds made from stone or bricks are more permanent than those that are made from wood planks. Except, you build a temporary garden by making use of a removable garden box. Simply set the box on the ground, place cardboard over the grass inside, and fill the box with soil. So that when you relocate, you can easily take the box with you and spread out the soil. However, make sure that you plan carefully before building your bed to reduce the possibility of having to move it later on.

Cost

The cost can be a bit of an issue, depending on the materials that you use for the raised bed garden. If you use low-cost materials or recycled materials to construct it, you minimize your cost, but you will still need lots of soil. Typically, having to purchase soil makes up the majority of the cost of building a raised bed garden. The majority of the costs of a raised bed garden happen at construction only. Once you have the bed, it takes very little, if any, cost to maintain. You can use purchased or homemade compost to fill the bed and reduce costs somewhat.

If you do have to purchase topsoil, then that will be another cost that you will have to consider. You also will want to consider purchasing some fertilizer to help the plants grow better.

Limitations of Equipment

The fact that the soil in a raised bed is loose and well-aerated is one of the benefits of a raised bed garden. Sadly, the soil quality and the construction of the raised bed garden limit the gardening equipment used in the maintenance of the bed. Heavy gardening equipment, such as power tillers, can't be used because they either don't' fit or they can ruin the quality of the soil. Raised bed gardens require you to use hand tools instead of power tools to cultivate the soil.

Work

When building and preparing a raised bed garden, you will expend much more effort than if you were preparing a traditional garden. You can hire someone to build it for you or purchase a pre-made one. Once you have filled it with soil, you can simply start planting.

Plan Well, or Plan to Fail

If you don't take the time to consider the requirements of the plants that you are planting, you will surely fail. You must make sure that you read your seed packages or your plant tags to be sure that you don't group together those plants that have different requirements. You don't want to put those shorter plants that need lots of sunlight with those tall plants that will end up shading them.

CONCLUSION

Gardening with raised beds can be very satisfying for even novice gardeners. The raised bed reduces the number of weeds and can make maintenance far easier especially for those with back or joint problems.

They also provide a more controlled environment for more sensitive plants, allowing you to maintain the PH and mineral balance in the soil more easily than planting directly into the ground. Be sure to plan out your garden correctly and it could provide you with years of pleasure with high yields of fresh fruits and vegetables or attractive flowers and plants.

By taking a little time to consider your raised bed garden, you are sure to create the perfect environment for your vegetables, ornamental flowers or other plants to flourish and look spectacular.

Made in the USA
San Bernardino, CA
21 July 2019